Watching Clouds

Julie Haydon

Contents

Watching Clouds	2
Mum's Job	5
What Are Clouds Made Of?	6
What Is Rain?	8
What Are Snow and Hail?	10
What Do Clouds Tell Us?	12
Can We Always See Clouds?	14
Glossary	16

Watching Clouds

Mum and I watched clouds in the sky, today.
The clouds were white.
The sky was blue.

The wind blew.
The wind made the clouds move and change shape.

I asked Mum about clouds and the weather.

Mum's Job

Mum's job is to tell people about the weather, every day.

She looks at photos of clouds on her **computer**.

What Are Clouds Made Of?

Some clouds are made of tiny drops of water.

Some clouds are made of tiny bits of ice.

Some clouds are made of tiny drops of water and tiny bits of ice.

What Is Rain?

Rain is big drops
of water
that falls from clouds.

The big drops of water
are made
of lots of tiny drops.

The big drops
are too heavy
to stay in the clouds.

What Are Snow and Hail?

Sometimes,
tiny bits of ice
fall from clouds.
This is called **snow**.

Bigger bits of ice that fall from clouds are called **hail**.

What Do Clouds Tell Us?

Some clouds
are white and puffy.
Clouds like this tell us
that the weather
will be fine.

Some clouds are big and dark. Clouds like this tell us that it will rain or snow or hail soon.

Can We Always See Clouds?

Sometimes,

we can not see any clouds.

Clouds can change a lot in a day.
It is fun to draw the pictures they make.

Glossary

computer

hail

snow